MARIE-PIERRE MOINE'S FRENCH KITCHEN

SOUPS AND VEGETABLES

LES POTAGES ET LEGUMES

ILLUSTRATED BY NADINE WICKENDEN

SIMON & SCHUSTER

New York   London   Toronto   Sydney   Tokyo   Singapore

For Norma Coates

SIMON & SCHUSTER
Rockefeller Center
1230 Avenue of the Americas
New York, New York 10020

Designed by Andrew Barron & Collis Clements Associates
Typesetting by Dorchester Typesetting in England
Printed and bound in Italy by New Interlitho

10 9 8 7 6 5 4 3 2 1

Library of Congress Cataloging in Publication Data
Available upon Request
ISBN: 0-671-89660-1

CONTENTS

INTRODUCTION

In towns all over France, the market, *le marché*, is the event of the week. Like a travelling circus, it brings color and excitement. It is the vegetables which give the stalls much of their vividness and opulence. Look one way and you see professional pyramids of firm bright tomatoes, pink potatoes, polished courgettes, darkly glinting aubergines, snow-white onions. Across the alleyway on a folding table there is a dishevelled mound of shallots, a few purple heads of garlic and a great bunch of carrots in need of a good scrub, still with their leafy fronds. Come midday when the heaps of ripe vegetables have disappeared into bags, and baskets, you start to feel hungry. Yet, when you examine the menu of the little restaurant across the square, you'll see very few mentions of vegetables – maybe *Salade de tomates, Soupe à l'oignon, Garniture de légumes,* or *Légumes du jour. Mais où sont les légumes du marché?* But where are the riches of the market? In bistros, brasseries and restaurants great and small, vegetables tend to disappear into garnishes, stocks and sauces. You could say that they have an image problem. . .

To enjoy the true riches of French vegetable cooking, you have to eat at home, *en famille*, with a French family who is not setting out to impress you with expensive animal protein – elaborately prepared meat or fish dishes.

Soup, the old heart of the meal, has remained a favourite way to start *le dîner*, dinner or supper – *le souper*. It can be rustic or elegant, rugged or smooth, a light first course or a substantial main meal, propped with a little meat, fish or seafood. It has many names, most of which are difficult to translate with a single word.

There is clear *bouillon*, sheer light stock, basic *soupe* and slightly more complex *potage*. *Crème* is puréed and cream-like in texture. More refined still is *velouté*, as smooth as velvet and often thickened with a mixture of cream and egg yolk. *Bisque* is a strained purée of seafood, vegetables and aromatics, enriched with cream, butter and alcohol.

The concept of 'meat and two veg' does not really exist in France. Vegetables, prepared simply but thoughtfully, tend to be passed around the table after the meat, fish or poultry is on the plates. The first vegetables of the season are eagerly awaited – almost like a new baby in the family.

Fresh vegetables are served a dish at a time in appetizing small amounts. This remains true when there is no meat or fish course. I have surprised many a visiting foreign friend by serving solo *Poêlée de champignons, Haricots verts persillés,* or *Gratin dauphinois* – pan-fried mixed mushrooms, buttery fresh green beans straight from the garden or a golden dish of creamy baked potatoes.

SOUPES ET POTAGES

SOUPS

FIRST PREPARE YOUR
BOUILLON . . .

Homemade chicken stock is hard to beat and I prepare it regularly (page 10). When I am caught without, and a recipe calls for *bouillon*, depending on what is required, working my way down from very good to 'most acceptable,' I use bought chilled stock if I can find it in the supermarket; a can of strained consommé; powdered stock from health food stores (less salty than ordinary big brands); last but not least, simply a little light soy sauce diluted in water – say 1 teaspoon in up to 5 tablespoons of water.

★　To prepare fine flavored *bouillon de légumes*, vegetable stock, add a few fennel seeds and extra herbs to the vegetable and flavoring mixture used to make chicken stock (page 10). Simmer for about 30 minutes and strain at once very thoroughly. Keep chilled for up to 3 or 4 days. The vegetables are delicious with *Rouille* (page 25) or Mornay sauce (page 36).

For making fish stock (*Bouillabaisse*) see page 24. If you simply want to poach fish, prepare a *court bouillon* by simmering a bouquet garni with a little extra thyme, a sprig of parsley, a few rings of onion, and strips of unwaxed lemon zest for about 15 minutes. Strain to remove and discard the flavorings.

POTAGE BONNE FEMME

WINTER VEGETABLE SOUP

Typical of *potage maison*, down-home soup as it is made in millions of kitchens all over France, this simple winter soup has to be generously seasoned. It is of course very flexible – celery and turnips being tasty options.

★   In a large heavy saucepan, heat the oil and melt half the butter over moderate heat. Add the vegetables and sauté for a few minutes. Season. Pour in about 1 quart boiling water. Add the bouquet garni and simmer for about 35 to 40 minutes, until the vegetables are cooked and tender.

Leave to cool for a few minutes, then remove the bouquet garni and process the soup in a blender or food processor. Strain through a sieve back into the pan, pushing well with the back of a wooden spoon. Stir in the stock. Adjust the seasoning, gently reheat. Just before serving, swirl in the rest of the butter and, if you like, a teaspoon of cream into each serving bowl.

Serves 4

2 tsp sunflower oil
4 tbsp butter
2 large waxy potatoes, peeled
3 leeks, washed, trimmed and chopped
2 carrots, peeled and chopped
1 Spanish onion, chopped
1 shallot, very finely chopped
1 bouquet garni
$\frac{1}{2}$ cup chicken or vegetable stock
4 tsp heavy cream, to serve, if liked
sea salt and freshly ground black pepper

BOUILLON DE POULET AUX FINES HERBES

CLEAR CHICKEN BROTH WITH HERBS

Serves 4

*2 carrots, peeled and
chopped
2 leeks, washed
¹/₂ small head of celery,
trimmed and chopped
1 onion, coarsely chopped
1 large chicken
1 bouquet garni
a few strips of unwaxed
lemon zest
6 black peppercorns
2 tbsp butter
4 large lettuce leaves, rolled
and snipped
6 spinach or sorrel leaves,
rolled and snipped
1 scallion, chopped
2 tbsp one or more of the
following finely snipped
fresh herbs: parsley, chives,
chervil, tarragon, plus 1
extra tbsp to finish
sea salt and freshly ground
black pepper*

Homemade *bouillon de poulet*, chicken stock, is light, fragrant, and clean-tasting. I remove the breast meat halfway through cooking before it turns too soft and serve it separately. Golden and clear, this great comfort food is perfect on its own but can be served with garlic croûtons.

Genuine chicken stock can be used in dozens of dishes and subtly improves sauces and soups. Since it takes a while to make and freezes extremely well, I make a double quantity from time to time and serve half on the day. If freezing some, after removing the chicken and flavorings, I boil up the clear stock until a little reduced, then let it go cold, remove the surface fat and decant it into small freezer bags. Not exactly pretty but very convenient for sauces.

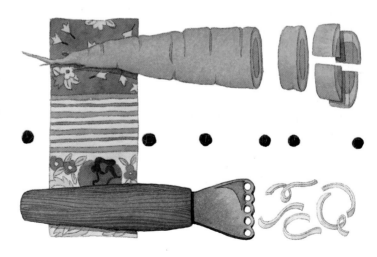

★   Make the chicken stock. Put the prepared vegetables in a large saucepan or cooking pot. Put the chicken on top. Season lightly, add the bouquet garni, lemon zest and peppercorns. Cover with about 2 quarts cold water and bring to a boil over low heat.

When the water starts to bubble, turn down the heat, and partially cover. Simmer for about 1 hour, skimming occasionally. Lift the chicken out. Cut off the breast-meat and serve hot or cold with a well seasoned mayonnaise. Put the remaining chicken back in the pot and continue simmering over low heat for 2 hours, skimming occasionally. Strain into a bowl, preferably through a cheesecloth-lined sieve. Leave to cool a little, then skim off the surface fat. Adjust the seasoning. The stock will keep for up to 3 days in the refrigerator. Discard the fatty top layer before using.

About 20 minutes before you are ready to serve, in a sauté pan, sweat the lettuce, spinach, scallion, and fresh herbs in the butter for a few minutes over low heat. Pour in the stock. Adjust the seasoning. Bring to low simmer. Simmer for 10 to 15 minutes.

Stir in the reserved snipped herbs. Adjust the seasoning and serve piping hot.

GRATINEE A L'OIGNON

ONION SOUP WITH A CHEESE CRUST

Serves 4

2 tsp sunflower oil
2 tbsp butter
1½ lb large sweet white
onions, thinly sliced
1 shallot, finely chopped
½ clove garlic, crushed
1 scant tbsp flour
1 bouquet garni
pinch of nutmeg
4 tsp brandy
8 thin slices of baguette-style
French bread
1 cup grated Gruyère
1 small egg yolk and 3 tbsp
heavy cream (optional)
sea salt and freshly ground
black pepper

When I make *soupe à l'oignon,* whenever possible I use sweet white onions (or even the white parts of a large bunch of scallions) rather than yellow Spanish onions which tend to be on the bitter side. The *liaison* of egg yolk and cream adds a smooth *soupçon* of luxury to this famous soup.

Gruyère is the classic cheese, but you can use mature Cheddar, Wensleydale or a mixture of Cheddar and blue cheese.

★ In a large sauté pan, combine the oil and butter over a moderate heat. Sauté the onion slices with the shallot and garlic until a little softened and golden, stirring frequently. Make sure they do not burn.

Stir in the flour and season. Pour in about 1 quart boiling water, add the bouquet garni and cook for about 20 minutes, stirring from time to time.

Heat the oven to 400°F. Spread some of the grated cheese over the bread slices. Put 1 prepared slice of bread in each of 4 oven-proof individual bowls or ramekins. Ladle in the onion soup, removing the bouquet garni. Adjust the seasoning, adding a tiny pinch of nutmeg and a teaspoon of brandy to each bowl.

Float a second slice of bread on each bowl, grated cheese on top. Put in the oven for about 10 minutes until golden and bubbling, then serve at once. If you like, mix the egg yolk with the cream and spoon a little of this mixture between the crust and the broth just before serving.

VELOUTE AUX CHAMPIGNONS

VELVETY MUSHROOM SOUP

If at all possible, use genuine chicken stock to prepare this smooth, rich soup (see page 10). *Velouté aux champignons* reheats well and makes a very reliable first course for a dinner party. The snipped *fines herbes* enhance both the flavor and the delicate beige color. Serve with fresh buttered toast.

★   In a sauté pan, melt half the butter over moderate heat. Stir in the shallots, mushrooms (reserving a large handful) and potato, season and cook gently for a few minutes, stirring frequently.

Pour in the chicken stock and bring to a simmer, stirring from time to time. Reduce the heat a little, cover, and cook gently for 20 to 25 minutes, stirring a few times. Meanwhile, in a small frying pan, sauté the reserved mushrooms in half the remaining butter for a few minutes. Sprinkle with the sherry and/or brandy and set aside.

Leave the soup to cool for a few minutes, then process in a blender or food processor. Return to the pan and adjust the seasoning.

In a bowl, mix the egg yolk with the cream, then stir in a ladleful of soup. Pour this *liaison* into the pan, stir well over low heat until piping hot. Add the sautéed mushrooms. Adjust the seasoning. Whisk in the rest of the butter and, if you like, sprinkle over the snipped herbs. Serve piping hot.

Serves 4

1 lb brown mushrooms, wiped and thinly sliced
2 shallots, finely chopped
1 large waxy potato, peeled and diced
4 tbsp butter
1 quart homemade chicken stock (page 10)
1 tbsp sherry and/or 2 tsp brandy
1 egg yolk
4 tbsp heavy cream
1 tbsp finely snipped parsley or chives (optional)
sea salt and freshly ground black pepper

GARBURE

CABBAGE, PORK, AND MEAT STEW

Serves 6

1 lb white haricot beans
4 slices of thick-cut smoked
bacon, rind removed and
chopped
1 lb smoked belly of pork,
chopped
1 bouquet garni
1 Spanish onion, chopped
2 carrots, peeled and
chopped
6 black peppercorns
3 cloves garlic, crushed
1 very large waxy potato, cut
into 8 chunks
1 Savoy cabbage, cored,
trimmed and quartered
1 small can of goose or duck
confit
sea salt and freshly ground
black pepper

This no-nonsense knife-and-fork stew comes from south west France and is a good example of gutsy one-pot country cooking. A small amount of *confit* – duck or goose cooked and preserved in its own fat, gives it a unique flavor. I prefer to finish it gratinée-style, in the oven or under the broiler but you can also put the bread, coated with mustard, in a heated tureen, pour the stew on top, and stir in the cheese.

★ Rinse the haricot beans. Put them in a large saucepan or cooking pot, cover with plenty of cold water. Bring to the boil and simmer for 10 minutes over moderate heat. Drain, rinse, and reserve.

In the same pot, blanch the pork and bacon in boiling water for a few minutes. Drain well. Rinse the pot. Put in the beans, pork, bacon, bouquet garni, onion, carrots, peppercorns, and

garlic. Cover with plenty of fresh water (about 1½ quarts). Bring to a simmer over a moderate heat. Season. Reduce the heat a little and simmer gently, half-covered, for about 1 hour, skimming from time to time.

Add the potato and cabbage, return to a simmer, and cook for another 30 minutes. Add the confit and a little of its fat. Stir, adjust the seasoning, and cook for a further 15 minutes.

Heat the broiler to high or, if you prefer, the oven to 400°F. Spread a little mustard over the bread. Place the slices on top of the stew, dunk in to moisten, then sprinkle with the grated cheese.

Reduce the heat a little and put under the broiler or in the oven for a few minutes until the cheese is bubbling and golden. Serve piping hot.

For the topping:

6 thick slices of slightly stale French country bread
1 tbsp coarse-grain or Dijon-style mustard
6 tbsp grated Gruyère or mature Cheddar

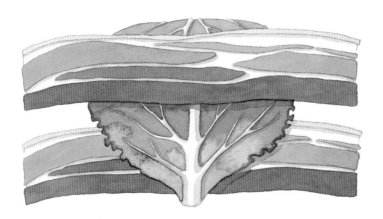

VELOUTE A LA TOMATE

WINTER TOMATO SOUP

Serves 4

2 tbsp butter
1 Spanish onion, finely chopped
1 leek, washed and sliced
1 carrot, peeled and chopped
a small head of celery, trimmed and chopped
6 large ripe tomatoes, blanched, seeded, skinned and chopped or 1 large can tomatoes
½ tsp each dried thyme and oregano
2 tsp finely snipped basil
1 heaped tbsp flour
1 quart light stock
1 egg yolk
4 tbsp heavy cream
sea salt and freshly ground black pepper

A *velouté* usually refers to a softened vegetable mixture blended with egg yolk and cream until velvet-like in texture. If the tomatoes available look water-logged and insipid, use a can or add a scant tablespoon of concentrate.

★ In a sauté pan, melt the butter over a moderate heat. Add the onion, leek, carrot, and celery. Season and sauté for 2 to 3 minutes, stirring frequently.

Stir in the tomatoes, the dried herbs, and half the basil. Cook for a minute, then sprinkle over the flour, stir, and cook for 2 to 3 minutes.

Now pour in the stock and bring to a simmer, stirring occasionally. Reduce the heat a little, partially cover, and cook over low heat for 20 to 25 minutes, stirring occasionally. Leave the soup to cool for a few minutes, then process in a blender or food processor. Return to the pan and adjust the seasoning.

In a bowl, mix the egg yolk with the cream, then stir in a ladleful of soup. Stir the mixture into the pan over a low heat until piping hot. Stir in the rest of the basil and serve immediately.

POTAGE A L'OSEILLE

SORREL SOUP

This sharpish green soup is perfect on a cold day in early spring. To turn it into a main course for a light supper or lunch, add a poached egg per guest to the soup just before serving. Follow the same recipe for spinach or watercress.

★ Heat the oil and half the butter in a sauté pan, then add the potato, sauté for a minute. Add the sorrel, spinach, or watercress and cook for a few minutes until wilted. Season lightly and stir in a little nutmeg.

Add the stock and bring to the boil. Reduce the heat, cover, and simmer for 20 minutes or until the potato is cooked. Leave to cool for a few minutes.

Pour into a blender or food processor and process until smooth. Strain the soup through a sieve back into the pan, pushing with the back of a wooden spoon.

Put over low heat. Whisk in the crème fraîche. Reheat until almost simmering, stirring occasionally. Stir in the grated cheese. Adjust the seasoning and whisk in the rest of the butter. Serve very hot, with toast or croûtons.

Serves 4

1 tbsp sunflower oil
3 tbsp butter
1 large waxy potato, peeled and diced
about 8 oz young sorrel leaves, or baby spinach leaves or trimmed watercress, rinsed
1/4 tsp nutmeg
1 quart light stock
3 tbsp crème fraîche
2 heaped tbsp grated Gruyère, mature Cheddar or similar
sea salt and freshly ground black pepper
toast or croûtons, to serve

SOUPE AU PISTOU

BROAD BEAN AND TOMATO SOUP WITH PESTO SAUCE

Serves 4

2 tbsp olive oil
1 Spanish onion, finely
chopped
2 cloves garlic, crushed
3½ cups vegetable (or
chicken) stock
1¼ lb fresh tomatoes,
blanched, seeded, skinned
and chopped or a large can
chopped tomatoes
1 tbsp snipped fresh basil
½ tsp each dried thyme,
sage and oregano
1 large waxy potato, diced
4 small turnips, peeled and
chopped
1 carrot, peeled and chopped
1 head fennel, trimmed and
chopped
4 small zucchini, chopped
12 oz shelled baby lima
beans (fresh or frozen)
a large handful broken up
vermicelli
croûtons, to serve
sea salt and freshly ground
black pepper

Intrigued by the word *pistou* hand-written on a slate over minuscule cuttings displayed on the ground in my local market (Amboise near Tours in the Loire valley – Friday and Sunday mornings, worth a detour) I asked the man who had brought them if I was right to assume it was basil, *du basilic*? *Bien sûr*, of course, he replied with a big grin. *Je le fais pousser pour mes nouilles. . .* I grow it for my noodles. *Pistou*, a pungent rough purée of fresh basil, garlic and olive oil and a favorite condiment of Provençal cooking, is gaining popularity in the rest of France along with the eating of pasta.

This hearty soup is one of my favorite meal-in-itself French vegetarian dishes. Feel free to vary the mix of ingredients: try adding red kidney beans, fresh green beans and a tablespoon of snipped parsley.

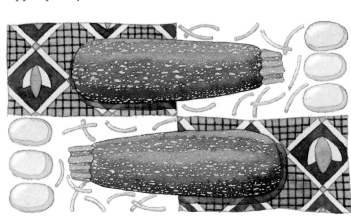

★ Heat the oil in a large sauté pan or cooking pot. Cook the onion and garlic over a moderate heat for 3 to 5 minutes, stirring frequently. Bring the stock to the boil in a separate pan.

Add the tomatoes with any juice, the basil, and dried herbs. Season and stir, then add the potato, turnips, and carrot. Pour in the boiling stock, stir, and return to the boil. As soon as the liquid bubbles, reduce the heat a little, add the fennel and zucchini, and season again lightly. Cover and simmer for about 15 minutes, stirring a few times.

Throw in the lima beans and vermicelli. Cook for a further 10 to 15 minutes until the vegetables are tender.

Prepare the Pistou sauce while the soup is simmering. Boil the egg for 4 minutes, then scoop out the yolk and put it in a bowl. Reserve the white. Beat the yolk with a pinch of salt, the mustard, garlic, and vinegar. Using an electric whisk, beat in the oil, a few drops at a time, then in a thin trickle, as if you were making a mayonnaise. Start with the groundnut oil, then work in the olive oil.

Mash up the egg white and stir into the sauce with the basil and cheese. Season generously.

To serve spoon some sauce into a heated soup tureen or individual bowls. Tilt to coat. Pour or ladle in the soup, spoon over the rest of the sauce and serve very hot with croûtons.

For the Pistou sauce:

1 egg
1 tsp Dijon-style mustard
1 clove garlic, crushed
1 tsp wine vinegar
1 cup oil (half a cup each of
groundnut oil and olive oil)
3 tbsp snipped fresh basil
5 tbsp grated strong Gruyère
or Parmesan cheese

SOUPE FRAICHE D'ETE

CHILLED TOMATO SOUP WITH HERBS AND AVOCADO

Serves 4

2¼ lb ripe tomatoes, rinsed
1 tbsp butter
1 clove garlic, crushed
1 sweet white onion, finely chopped
a few drops of Tabasco
¼ tsp dried ground cumin
¼ tsp dried ground coriander
1 quart homemade chicken stock (page 10)
1 large ripe avocado, chopped
1½ tbsp lemon juice
1 tbsp finely snipped chives
2 tsp finely snipped tarragon or parsley or chervil
sea salt and freshly ground black pepper

This is a Moine preparation, engineered in the kitchen of the family house in the Loire valley one day, when I was trying to use up a heap of over-ripe tomatoes from the garden. With its satiny texture and nicely acidic finish, I can best describe this chilled soup as a happy compromise between a vichyssoise and a gazpacho.

★ Process the tomatoes in a blender or food processor. Strain well, using the back of a wooden spoon to push the purée through a fine sieve into a bowl. Set aside.

In a small frying pan, melt the butter over a moderate heat. Add the garlic, onion, Tabasco, cumin, and coriander. Season generously and sauté for 2 to 3 minutes, stirring frequently. Take off the heat. Spoon in a little stock and stir well.

Pour the mixture into the blender or food processor. Process, then add the rest of the stock, the chopped avocado and lemon juice. Process until smooth.

Mix with the tomato purée. Adjust the seasoning. Stir in the fresh herbs. Refrigerate for 30 minutes or until needed. Taste and adjust the seasoning one more time. Serve chilled, diluted with a few ice cubes.

CREME AUX ASPERGES

CREAM OF ASPARAGUS SOUP

Bring about 3½ cups lightly salted water to the boil in a sauté pan. Add the asparagus, return to a simmer and cook for 5 to 7 minutes, until the tips are cooked. Lift out the asparagus. Cut out and reserve 12 tips. Return the rest to the pan and continue cooking for 10 to 15 minutes until soft. Drain well, reserving the cooking liquid.

In the pan, now melt the butter over a moderate heat. Sauté the onion and shallot with the dried tarragon for 5 minutes, stirring frequently, until softened. Sprinkle with the flour and cook for a minute, stirring frequently.

Whisk in the reserved liquid, a little at a time. Bring to a simmer with the asparagus stalks. Continue cooking for a minute or two, then leave to cool a little.

Process until smooth in a blender or food processor. Strain back into the pan, pushing the mixture through a sieve with a wooden spoon. Return to a low heat, add the wine and milk, and adjust the seasoning. Stir in the cream and reserved asparagus. Heat through. If you like, stir in the fresh tarragon. Serve hot.

Serves 4

at least 1 lb asparagus,
washed and trimmed
4 tbsp butter
½ sweet white onion or
white parts of 2 large
scallions, finely chopped
1 shallot, finely chopped
1 tsp dried tarragon
1 heaped tbsp flour
4 tbsp milk
4 tbsp dry white wine
3 tbsp light cream
1 tbsp finely snipped fresh
tarragon (optional)
sea salt and freshly ground
black pepper

PETITE BISQUE DE CREVETTES

CREAMY SHRIMP SOUP

Serves 4

1½ tbsp oil
2½ lb unpeeled large raw
shrimp, heads reserved
1 large soft white onion, very
finely chopped
2 shallots, very finely
chopped
1 clove garlic, crushed
3 tbsp brandy
3 tbsp short-grain rice
3 to 4 large ripe tomatoes,
blanched, seeded, skinned
and chopped or a large can of
tomatoes
1 bouquet garni
1 pint light fish stock
1 cup white wine
a pinch of saffron
cayenne pepper
paprika
4 tbsp crème fraîche, plus a
little extra to finish
(optional)
2 tbsp chilled diced butter
2 tbsp finely snipped parsley
or chives (optional)
sea salt and freshly ground
black pepper

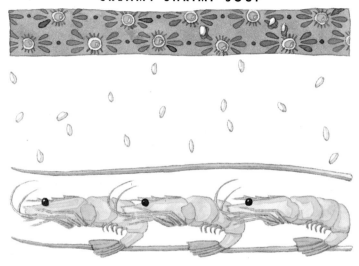

Whereas *bouillabaisse* was first boiled up by fishermen to use up the unsold remnants of the day's catch, the unctuous spicy *bisque* probably evolved in a medieval kitchen.

This most elegant and satisfying soup is unfortunately an expensive dish to prepare. In the recipe below I use raw shrimp, but the same method can be applied to lobster, langoustines, crab, and crayfish. What matters is that you crush the shells really well to extract as much flavor as possible. If you are using hard-shelled crustaceans, line the sieve with cheesecloth to catch treacherous tiny shell pieces.

★   Heat the oil in a large sauté pan over moderate heat. Add the shrimp and heads, and the prepared onion, garlic, and shallots. Sauté for a few minutes, stirring and smashing the shrimp heads with a large wooden spoon.

Sprinkle with half the brandy. Carefully set alight with a long match. Stir in the rice, tomatoes and juices, bouquet garni, fish stock, and wine. Season lightly and add a pinch of saffron and a small pinch each of cayenne and paprika. Bring back to a simmer.

Leaving the shrimp heads in the pan, lift out the bodies of the shrimp. Leave to cool while you continue to cook the other ingredients for 15 to 20 minutes over a moderate heat, stirring from time to time.

When they are cool enough to handle, shell the shrimp and reserve the flesh. Throw the shells back into the pan and stir to mix. Leave the soup to cool for 10 to 15 minutes. Neatly cut the cooked shrimp into small segments.

Lift out and discard the bouquet garni and heads. Process the soup and shells in a blender or food processor until smooth. Strain back into the pan, pushing the mixture through a fine sieve.

Place the pan over low heat. Add the rest of the brandy. Stir in the crème fraîche and the pieces of cooked shrimp. Adjust the seasoning. Whisk in the chilled butter.

Serve piping hot in heated soup bowls, preferably with a sprinkling of parsley and a swirl of crème fraîche.

BOUILLABAISSE MAISON

MEDITERRANEAN FISH STEW

Serves 6

4 tbsp fruity olive oil
1½ Spanish onions, finely chopped
3 cloves garlic, crushed
½ small fennel bulb, trimmed and chopped into small pieces and 2 tsp fennel seeds
about 2½ lb mixed filleted or skinned non-oily fish, preferably including a few pieces of strong flavored fish, cut into chunks, heads and parings reserved
1½ cups large raw shrimp, shells and heads reserved
4 large ripe tomatoes, blanched, seeded, skinned and chopped or a large can of tomatoes, drained
1 bouquet garni
a generous pinch of powdered saffron
4 strips of unwaxed orange peel
2 tbsp brandy or pastis
1 pint small mussels, well scrubbed and beards removed
sea salt and freshly ground black pepper
croûtons, to serve

I cannot promise that this dish will transport you straight to the heart or rather the sea front of old Marseilles, but the recipe below does produce a satisfactory *Bouillabaisse*. Be generous with the saffron, fennel, and garlic and use plenty of hot chili paste in the *Rouille*. The other important thing is to enlist your fish store's help – get plenty of heads and trimmings from non-oily fish and crustaceans for the stock.

★ In a large cooking pot, heat 1 tablespoon of olive oil and sauté half the onion with a little of the prepared garlic and fennel. Season lightly, cook for a few minutes over a moderate heat. Add the fish heads and parings, and the shrimp shells and heads, stir for a few minutes over moderate heat. Cover with plenty of boiling water (use at the very least 1 quart) and cook for 15 minutes. Push through a fine sieve with the back of a wooden spoon and reserve the liquid.

Heat 2 tablespoons of olive oil. Add the rest of the onion and the tomatoes, season lightly, and sauté for a few minutes over a moderate heat. Add the rest of the fennel and garlic, the bouquet garni, saffron, and orange peel. Stir and cook for 2 minutes.

Pour in the reserved liquid and the brandy or pastis and bring to the boil. Throw in the mussels (discarding any that are still open at this stage), then put the fish and shrimp on top. Season, stir and bring to the boil over moderate heat. Boil for 8 to 10 minutes.

Make the *Rouille* while the fish is boiling. In a bowl, mix the chili paste, moistened bread, crushed garlic, and egg yolk. Season.

Using an electric whisk, whisk in a few drops of oil, as if making mayonnaise. Continue dribbling in the oil very slowly, whisking constantly until the sauce thickens, then trickle it in more rapidly, still whisking. Adjust the seasoning.

Now serve the *Bouillabaisse* – each guest should have a heated wide soup bowl. Discard any mussels that haven't opened and, if you like, some of the top shells. Strain the cooking liquid into a heated pitcher. Heap the fish, mussels and prawns on a heated platter. Moisten with a few tablespoons of cooking liquid. Have the *Rouille* and plenty of croûtons on the table.

For the Rouille:

2 tsp chili paste
1 slice of soft bread, crust removed, broken into pieces, moistened with milk
2 to 3 cloves garlic, crushed
1 large very fresh egg yolk
³/₄ cup olive oil
sea salt and freshly ground black pepper

LEGUMES FRAIS

FRESH VEGETABLES

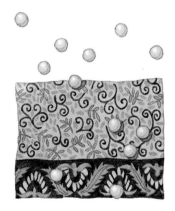

HARICOTS VERTS PERSILLES

GREEN BEANS WITH PARSLEY

Serves 4

*1 lb young green beans,
topped and tailed
1 clove garlic, halved
2 tbsp butter
2 tbsp finely snipped parsley
sea salt and freshly ground
black pepper*

To this day the sight of a plateful of freshly picked green beans anointed with butter and parsley makes my mouth water. *Haricots verts* were daily fare during summer holidays in the Loire valley. What we could not consume on the spot we bottled or took to be canned in a very primitive local factory. Tailing and topping was done by hand, bean after bean, sitting in the sun in the garden and gossiping. It was only years later that I discovered that the best way to top and tail was to take a handful of beans, knock them level on the work surface, then snip them with kitchen scissors.

★ Remove any strings and break up the larger beans. Season a large saucepan of boiling water with salt .

Throw in the beans, bring back to a rolling boil and keep bubbling over a high heat until the beans are cooked through and just tender – this will take 4 to 8 minutes depending on the beans.

Drain the beans and plunge them into a bowl of iced water. Drain again after a few seconds. Spread on a double layer of paper towels to dry.

Now rub a frying pan with the cut sides of the garlic. Melt the butter over a moderate heat. Add the beans to the sizzling butter. Stir until well coated, then sprinkle over the parsley. Stir, adjust the seasoning, and serve as soon as possible.

POELEE DE CHAMPIGNONS

PAN-FRIED MUSHROOMS

Serves 4

1¼ lb mixed mushrooms,
wiped and sliced, if necessary
1 clove garlic, halved
1½ tbsp oil
3 tbsp butter
1 shallot, finely chopped
2 tbsp finely snipped parsley
or chives or chervil
sea salt and freshly ground
black pepper

Life in the kitchen is a continuous education. For this recipe's little *truc*, the trick of twice-cooking mushrooms, I am indebted to my father who some time ago convinced me that it was a good way to get rid of some excess moisture. Make the most of the exciting selection of mushrooms now widely available in good supermarkets and markets.

★ Rub a sauté pan or frying pan with the cut sides of garlic. Pour the oil into the pan and tilt the pan around over a moderate heat to spread the oil. Add the mushrooms to the hot oil, season lightly and sauté for 5 to 7 minutes, stirring occasionally.

Spread the mushrooms over a big plate lined with a double layer of paper towels. Cover with more paper towels and leave for a few minutes to drain.

Wipe the sauté pan and put it over a moderate heat. Melt half the butter. Crush the garlic. Add the shallots, garlic and a table-spoon of herbs to the pan. Stir for 2 minutes, then add the mush-rooms and spread them well in the pan. Turn up the heat a fraction, season generously and sauté for 5 minutes.

Stir in the rest of the butter and herbs. Adjust the seasoning and serve hot.

GRATIN DE LEGUMES A LA PROVENÇALE

BAKED MEDITERRANEAN VEGETABLES

Serves 4 as a main course, 6 to 8 as a side dish

at least 6 tbsp fruity olive oil
3 to 4 unblemished ripe eggplant, thinly cut
2 red bell peppers
1 yellow bell pepper
6 medium-to-large ripe tomatoes
2 large sweet white onions, cut into thin rings
1 or more cloves garlic, crushed
½ tsp each of: dried thyme, marjoram, oregano and summer sweet savory, all mixed together
2 tbsp finely snipped fresh basil
12 black olives, pitted and halved
3 tbsp grated Gruyère or mature Cheddar (optional)
sea salt and freshly ground black pepper

This colorful dish is sometimes called *tian*, after the earthenware pot the cooks of Provence traditionally bake it in. Splendid party food, this gratin can be prepared the night before, baked the next day and left to cool – it will taste just as good *tiède*, tepid (sounds better in French), or even at room temperature.

★ Heat 2 tablespoons of olive oil in a large frying-pan. Sauté the eggplant slices a few at a time over a moderate heat. Turn over the slices the moment they become golden on the outside. Once they are colored on both sides, spread the slices on a double layer of paper towels, turn over and pat dry with more paper to absorb as much of the fat as possible.

Continue until all the eggplant are sautéed, adding oil as necessary. You will need to reduce the heat after a batch or two to make sure the eggplant do not burn – this step requires a little patience.

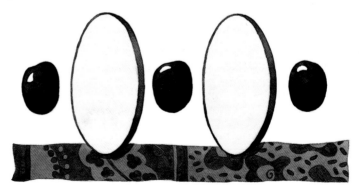

While you are browning the eggplant, char the peppers under the broiler or directly over a flame. Leave to cool a little once they have blistered, then peel off the skin, seed, core, and cut into thin strips. Also blanch the tomatoes in boiling water. Skin, slice, and remove the seeds and excess pulp.

In the frying pan, sauté the onion rings with the garlic and a teaspoon of mixed dried herbs over moderate heat for a few minutes until softened and golden. Season.

Heat the oven to 350°F. Lightly oil a gratin dish. Spread in a layer of sautéed eggplant slices. Season lightly and sprinkle with a pinch of dried herbs and some snipped basil. Spread over the tomato slices and the onion mixture. Scatter over the black olives. Season, sprinkle with herbs and basil. Cover with the bell pepper strips. Season as before and top with the rest of the eggplant. Sprinkle this final layer with the rest of the dried herbs and basil and a little more olive oil.

Bake for about 50 minutes. If you like, take out of the oven and sprinkle over the cheese. In any case increase the heat to 400°F for the last 10 minutes of cooking. Leave to cool and serve warm rather than hot.

TOMATES A LA PROVENÇALE

BAKED TOMATOES WITH HERBS

Serves 4

8 firm ripe medium tomatoes
2 tbsp fruity olive oil
1 or 2 cloves garlic, crushed
1 scallion, finely snipped
3 tbsp finely snipped fresh
herbs chosen from the
following: parsley, chervil,
chives and tarragon
1 tsp dried ground thyme
1 tsp of 1 or more of the
following: oregano,
marjoram, sweet savory, sage
2 tbsp fresh bread crumbs or
pine nuts
1 tsp sugar (optional)
2 tbsp butter, diced
sea salt and freshly ground
black pepper

Good enough to be a separate course in its own right. If you haven't got access to an exciting selection of fresh herbs, make up for it with dried herbs – they'll have plenty of time to mellow inside the moist tomatoes during cooking. The minimalist stuffing also works nicely with baked bell peppers. Halve, core and seed before cooking.

★ Cut off the tops of the tomatoes. Using a pointed small teaspoon, scoop out the seeds and pale pulp without breaking the skin. Leave in as much flesh as possible.

Sprinkle a little salt inside the tomatoes. Put upside down on a plate and leave to drain for about 30 minutes.

Heat the oven to 350°F. Heat half the olive oil in a small frying pan and sauté the garlic and scallion over moderate heat for 2 minutes.

Put the sautéed garlic and scallion in a bowl. Mix in the herbs and bread crumbs or pine nuts. Season. If you like, add a teaspoon of sugar.

Gently press the tomatoes to finish draining and fill them with the garlic mixture, using the teaspoon. Adjust the seasoning and put a few dice of butter on the top of each tomato.

Using a small wad of paper towels, oil a gratin dish just large enough to take the tomatoes side by side. Put in the tomatoes and bake in the oven for about 50 minutes or longer. The tomatoes should be soft but not mushy – check after 35 minutes and reduce the heat a little if necessary. Leave to cool a little before serving.

EPINARDS AU BEURRE

LEAF SPINACH WITH BUTTER

S pinach is a versatile vegetable partner, equally at home with egg dishes, broiled red meats, fish, and seafood. I prefer it with butter only when I serve it with steak but the creamy version is perfect with egg and seafood dishes.

★　Blanch the spinach for 1 minute in lightly salted boiling water. Drain well, refresh under cold water, and drain again. Squeeze gently a handful at a time to extract as much moisture as possible and spread on a double layer of paper towels.

Melt half the butter in a sauté pan over moderate heat. Add the spinach and a pinch of nutmeg, season, and stir.

Sauté for 2 to 3 minutes, stirring frequently. Cut the rest of the butter into dice and dot over the spinach. Cook as before for 1 minute.

If you like, while the spinach is cooking, cook the cream in a small saucepan over moderate heat until reduced by half. Stir the reduced cream into the spinach, adjust the seasoning, and serve as soon as possible.

Serves 4

8 oz young leaf spinach, picked and trimmed
4 tbsp chilled butter
a small pinch of ground nutmeg
½ cup light cream (optional)
sea salt and freshly ground black pepper

PETITS POIS A L'ETUVEE

STEWED BABY PEAS

Serves 4

*3 tbsp butter
leaves from a small head of
lettuce, rolled and snipped
white parts of 3 scallions,
finely snipped
1 lb shelled petits pois or
tender baby garden peas
(about 4 lb unshelled peas)
½ cup chicken or vegetable
stock
1 tbsp snipped parsley or
mint leaves
sea salt and freshly ground
black pepper*

This very French way to cook freshly picked and just podded baby peas also works wonders on frozen peas and drained canned peas. If you like, stir into the finished dish a few spoonfuls of tiny lardons – small pieces of blanched and sautéed smoked bacon.

★ In a sauté pan, melt half the butter over a moderate heat. Add the scallions, and the lettuce strips (reserving a few lettuce pieces to finish off the dish). Sauté for 2 to 3 minutes.

Throw in the petits pois, season lightly, and pour in the stock. Bring to a simmer, then reduce the heat a fraction, cover, and simmer gently until the petits pois are tender – about 15 minutes depending on the peas.

Pour into a heated serving dish. Adjust the seasoning. Stir in the rest of the butter, a few more tiny strips of lettuce and the snipped parsley or mint. Serve hot.

NAVETS GLACES

GLAZED BABY TURNIPS

A pretty way to cook turnips and a favorite French *garniture*, accompaniment for duck and lamb. Follow the same recipe to prepare mature carrots and pearl onions.

★   Spread the turnips in a sauté pan in single layer. Season and sprinkle with sugar. Pour in just enough boiling water to cover. Distribute half the butter over the turnips. Bring back to a simmer.

Loosely cover the pan with a layer of foil, then cook over moderate heat until the water has evaporated and the turnips are just tender – this will take about 20 minutes.

Turn up the heat a fraction, remove the foil, and scatter half the remaining butter in the pan. Leave the turnips to turn golden brown, gradually adding the rest of the butter. Shake the pan frequently and turn over the turnips from time to time. Allow 15 to 20 minutes and keep an eye on the pan.

A minute or two before serving, sprinkle the parsley over the turnips and stir well.

Serves 4

1½ tbsp oil
8 tbsp butter
about 1¾ lb unblemished baby turnips, neatly trimmed and peeled
2 tsp sugar
1 tbsp finely snipped parsley
sea salt and freshly ground black pepper

35

CHOU-FLEUR MORNAY

CAULIFLOWER WITH CREAM AND CHEESE SAUCE

Serves 2 as a main course,
4 as a side dish

1 cauliflower
2 tbsp butter

For the Sauce Mornay
(makes just over 1 cup):

3 tbsp butter
1 heaped tbsp flour
1 cup milk
½ tsp dried ground thyme
small pinch of ground nutmeg
2 tbsp light cream
2 heaped tbsp grated Gruyère or mature Cheddar
pinch of paprika
sea salt and freshly ground black pepper

S ometimes I cook the cauliflower whole, having first trimmed its base and core, then pour the delicate Mornay sauce over it and serve without further ado.

★ Cut the cauliflower into small neat florets of more or less the same size. Bring a saucepan of water to the boil, season with salt, add the cauliflower florets and bring back to the boil. Reduce the heat a little and simmer for 8 to 10 minutes or until barely tender. Drain the florets, refresh under cold water, and set aside in a colander while you make the Mornay sauce.

Melt two-thirds of the butter in a saucepan over low heat. Add the flour and stir with a wooden spoon for about 40 seconds to make a pale roux. Gradually whisk in the milk. Season and sprinkle in the thyme and nutmeg. Bring to a simmer, still whisking steadily.

As soon as bubbles start to appear, reduce the heat. Simmer gently for about 10 to 12 minutes, stirring regularly, until the sauce thickens. Now add the cream, whisking to mix it in. Stir in the cheese and adjust the seasoning.

Heat the broiler until hot. Spread the cauliflower into a flameproof dish. Spoon over the Mornay sauce. Season lightly with a little extra pepper and the paprika. Dot with the rest of the butter and broil for a few minutes until bubbly and golden. Leave to cool just a little before serving.

ENDIVES AU JAMBON
BELGIAN ENDIVE BAKED WITH HAM

A supper dish I grew up with. Use exactly the same method to prepare leeks. If you decide to leave out the ham, sprinkle a little lemon juice over the endive before cooking – this will help keep it looking bright.

★ Heat the oven to 350°F. Use some of the butter to grease a gratin dish just large enough to take the endive in a single layer.

Put the endive side by side in the dish. Sprinkle with sugar and wine, sage, and paprika and season lightly. Dot with half of the remaining butter and cover loosely with foil. Bake in the oven for about 30 minutes.

In a cup mix the Gruyère and crème fraîche. Season with a little black pepper.

Take the dish out of the oven and remove the foil. Leave until just cool enough to handle. Turn up the heat to 400°F.

Roll 1 slice of ham around each head of endive. Now spread the crème fraîche or cream and cheese mixture over the lot, dot with butter and return the dish to the oven.

Bake for a further 15 minutes, until golden and bubbling. Leave to cool for a few minutes and serve while still hot.

Serves 2 as a main course,
4 as a side dish

6 heads of Belgian endive,
washed and trimmed
4 tbsp butter
1 tsp sugar
1 tbsp sweet fortified wine
such as Madeira, port, or
sherry
1 tsp dried ground sage
small pinch of paprika
6 thin slices of roasted or
smoked ham
3 tbsp crème fraîche or heavy
cream
2 heaped tbsp grated
Gruyère or mature Cheddar
sea salt and freshly ground
black pepper

PAUPIETTES DE CHOU

STUFFED CABBAGE LEAVES

Serves 4 as a main course

*12 large unblemished leaves
from a large Savoy cabbage
1 cup vegetable or chicken
stock mixed with the same
amount of water
½ cup white wine
a few strips of unwaxed
lemon zest
1 bouquet garni
2 tbsp butter
2 tbsp crème fraîche*

For the filling:

*1 tbsp olive oil
1 tbsp butter
½ Spanish onion, finely
chopped
1 red bell pepper, cored,
seeded and finely chopped
1 cup button mushrooms,
finely sliced
1 clove garlic, crushed
¼ tsp chili paste
½ tsp finely grated lemon
zest
2 tbsp chopped shelled
pistachios
1 cup boiled rice or cooked
bulgur
1 egg
sea salt and freshly ground
black pepper*

Paupiettes are parcels of meat or vegetable leaves wrapped around a savory stuffing. In the recipe below I fill cabbage leaves with a well seasoned vegetarian stuffing and steam them over fragrant stock. Perfect for nutritionally correct guests. Use only the largest outer leaves from a curly green cabbage – you may need 2 cabbages.

★ Blanch the cabbage leaves for 2 minutes in lightly salted

boiling water. Drain well. Reserve on a double layer of paper towels while you prepare the filling.

Heat the oil and butter in a frying pan. Over a moderate heat, sauté the onion with the red pepper, mushrooms, garlic, chili paste, lemon zest, and pistachios for 5 minutes, stirring frequently.

Add to a bowl. Mix in the cooked rice, then the egg. Season generously.

Spoon the mixture into the center of the cabbage leaves. Roll into neat parcels, starting with the short sides which you bring in above the stuffing. Secure with string.

Bring to the boil the stock with the wine, lemon strips, and bouquet garni. Spread half the butter over the cabbage parcels. Place these in a steamer, steaming basket, or metal colander, cover tightly and steam for about 30 minutes over the bubbling liquid. Keep an eye on the liquid level and top up with water if necessary.

Just before serving, make a sauce in a small saucepan over a low heat. Mix ½ cup of cooking liquid with the crème fraîche. Season and whisk in the rest of the butter.

Cut off and discard the strings, and serve the cabbage parcels piping hot and moistened with the sauce.

CHAMPIGNONS FARCIS

BAKED STUFFED MUSHROOMS

Serves 4

*4 large undamaged flat
Portabello mushrooms
1 or 2 cloves garlic, crushed
2 tbsp finely snipped parsley
or chives
1 tsp dried thyme
1 thick slice slightly stale
bread, cut into 4, crust
removed
4 tbsp butter, or a little more
if preferred
a pinch of paprika
1½ tsp finely grated lemon
zest
4 tbsp light cream
4 tbsp dry white wine
sea salt and freshly ground
black pepper*

Make sure the mushrooms fit very tightly in the gratin dish or dishes – they shrink a little during cooking and the cream will evaporate if it is not protected by the mushrooms – which would be a pity. . . The delicious stuffing can also be used with mussels and large clams, or as a topping. Use as much garlic and butter as your conscience will let you.

★ Heat the oven to 400°F. Remove the stems from the mushrooms and break up into pieces. In a food processor, process the stem pieces with the garlic, herbs, bread, and half the butter. Scrape off the sides of the bowl and season generously, adding a tiny pinch of paprika and the lemon zest. Whizz again briefly.

Spoon the stuffing into the mushrooms. Spread well with a spatula. Halve the rest of the butter. Divide one half between the mushroom cups.

Butter 4 individual gratin dishes or a dish just big enough to take the mushrooms side by side. Mix the cream and wine in a cup and spoon this into the dishes or dish. Add the mushrooms. Bake for about 10 minutes, then reduce the heat to 325°F, and continue baking for 15 minutes or until the filling is bubbling and the mushrooms are softened. If you like, broil for a few minutes just before serving. Serve piping hot, with plenty of bread.

COURGETTES SAUTEES

SAUTÉED ZUCCHINI WITH THYME

Select your zucchini carefully for this dish – they should be on the small side but not tiny, firm and unblemished. If I have used only olive oil and no butter, I sometimes sprinkle the sautéed zucchini with a little lemon juice and serve them at room temperature. Sharpen up at the last minute with extra oil, lemon juice, and seasoning.

★ Blanch the zucchini for 2 minutes in plenty of lightly salted boiling water. Drain, refresh under cold water, and drain again. Spread on a clean dish towel or double paper towels and press dry to absorb as much moisture as you can from the zucchini.

Rub a large frying pan with the cut side of the garlic. Add the oil and put over a moderate heat. Add half the butter. When the butter has melted, spread the zucchini in the pan. Crush the garlic, add to the pan with the thyme and scallion. Season and cook for 5 to 7 minutes.

Turn over the zucchini slices with a spatula or fish slice – the underside should be golden. Add the rest of the butter, turn down the heat a fraction and cook as before for another 5 to 7 minutes. If you like, pat with paper towels to absorb excess fat just before serving. Adjust the seasoning and eat hot or warm.

Serves 4

1 lb ripe small to medium zucchini, rinsed and thinly sliced (but not wafer thin)
½ clove garlic, or more, if liked
1½ tbsp olive oil
2 tbsp butter (or an extra 2 tbsp olive oil)
1 tsp dried ground thyme
1 scallion, snipped
sea salt and freshly ground black pepper

POMMES DE TERRE

POTATOES

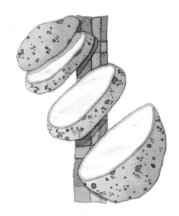

POMMES DE TERRE SAUTEES AUX FINES HERBES

SAUTÉED POTATOES WITH HERBS

Serves 4

1 lb potatoes, peeled and cut into thick slices
1 clove garlic, halved
3 or more tbsp groundnut or olive oil
½ tsp each dried thyme and rosemary
2 tbsp finely snipped parsley or chives
2 tbsp butter
sea salt and freshly ground black pepper

Pommes *de terre sautées* are popular fare in France and a classic accompaniment for omelets, steaks, and roasts. For a luxurious main course medley, serve with *Haricots verts persillés* or *Poêlée de champignons* and sautéed *lardons*.

★ Put the potatoes in a sauté pan. Cover them with plenty of boiling water – there should be at least 1 inch of water above the potatoes. Season with salt and return to the boil over a high heat.

Reduce the heat to a fast simmer and par-boil the potatoes for 12 to 15 minutes, until they are half cooked.

Drain well and leave in a colander to let off steam for a little while.

Rub the pan with the cut sides of the garlic. Heat half the oil until very hot. Cut the potato slices into wedges. Season and spread in the pan.

Cook for 3 minutes without stirring. Sprinkle over the thyme and rosemary and a tablespoon of fresh herbs. Stir well, reduce the heat a little, add the remaining oil, and continue cooking the potatoes for 7 to 10 minutes, stirring and turning over a fairly high heat until they are crisp and brown. Shake the pan from time to time and keep an eye on the heat.

Just before serving, stir in the butter, adjust the seasoning, and scatter over the rest of the fresh herbs. Serve very hot.

PUREE DE POMMES DE TERRE

CREAMED POTATOES

A universal favorite. Use a vegetable mill or a potato ricer to mash the potatoes as delicately as possible and keep the starch unbroken.

★ Bring to the boil plenty of water in a large pan. Season with salt, drop in the potatoes, and return to the boil over a high heat.

As soon as the water bubbles, reduce the heat to a fast simmer. Cook the potatoes for 20 to 30 minutes, until they are done but not soft – the timing depends on the potatoes. Do not overcook and keep the simmering low and steady.

Drain well and leave the potatoes in a colander until cool enough to handle. Meanwhile, melt half the butter in the pan, add the nutmeg, then stir in the cream and the milk. Season, cook for 2 to 3 minutes over low heat, then pour into a jug.

Peel off their skins, then mash the potatoes. Work as lightly as possible in order not to make the purée too sticky.

Put the mashed potatoes in the pan. Off the heat, whisk in the cream mixture. Return the pan to low heat, whisk in the rest of the butter, a dice at a time. If the purée looks too stiff, stir in a little extra milk or cream. Adjust the seasoning and serve hot. The purée will keep nicely warm for up to 20 minutes over a pan of very hot water.

Serves 4

1¼ lb starchy potatoes, peeled
4 tbsp chilled diced butter
a tiny pinch of ground nutmeg
2 or more tbsp light or heavy cream
4 or more tbsp milk
sea salt and freshly ground black pepper

GRATIN DAUPHINOIS

POTATOES BAKED WITH MILK AND CREAM

Serves 6

*1³/₄ lb large starchy potatoes,
peeled and thinly sliced
1 clove garlic, halved
1 tbsp soft butter for greasing
and 2 tbsp chilled diced
butter
1¹/₄ cups whole milk
1 cup light cream
1 egg yolk
small pinch of ground
nutmeg
¹/₂ tsp dried ground thyme
1 tbsp finely snipped chives
or 1 small scallion, finely
snipped
4 tbsp grated Gruyère or
mature Cheddar
sea salt and freshly ground
black pepper*

This wonderful classic *gratin* is a treat with roasts but I almost prefer to enjoy it on its own.

★ Heat the oven to 350°F. Rub a round ceramic flan dish or a gratin dish with the cut sides of the garlic, then crush the clove and reserve. Grease the dish with butter.

Over low heat, mix the milk and cream in a saucepan. Season and stir in the nutmeg and ground thyme. Whisk in the egg yolk, crushed garlic, and finely snipped chives or scallion.

Pat the potatoes dry with a clean dish towel or paper towels. Spread a layer of potatoes in the prepared dish, half overlapping them. Season lightly. Spoon a little seasoned milk and cream over the potatoes. Repeat until you have used all the potatoes, making

sure you top the whole thing with a generous amount of milk and cream mixture. Distribute the diced butter over the surface of the dish.

Bake in the oven for about 50 minutes, then turn up the heat to 400°F. If you like, take the gratin out of the oven and sprinkle with the grated cheese. Continue baking for another 20 minutes, until the gratin is golden and the potatoes are tender – test them with a metal skewer. If the potatoes aren't quite ready, reduce the heat a little and bake for a further 10 to 15 minutes.

Serve hot or warm from the dish after leaving to cool for several minutes. If you can't serve within 20 minutes or so of baking, cover with foil, and keep warm in the switched off oven.

GRATIN AUX ECHALOTES

POTATOES BAKED WITH SHALLOTS AND BLUE CHEESE

Serves 6

1³/₄ lb large starchy potatoes, peeled and thinly sliced
¹/₂ clove garlic
1 tbsp soft butter for greasing and 4 tbsp butter, cut into slivers
1 tbsp groundnut or sunflower oil
3 shallots, finely chopped
8 oz brown mushrooms, wiped and thinly sliced or 4 large canned artichoke hearts, well drained and thinly sliced
1¹/₄ cups chicken or vegetable stock
¹/₂ cup dry white wine
at least 3 tbsp grated or slivered Bleu d'Auvergne, Fourme d'Ambert or other strong creamy blue cheese
salt and freshly ground black pepper

For a lighter dish, try baking the potatoes in stock. *Gratin aux échalotes* is a delicious cousin of *Gratin dauphinois* from the slimmer branch of the family. In this variation, I add shallots, mushrooms and a blue cheese topping.

★ Heat the oven to 350°F. Rub a round ceramic flan dish or a gratin dish with the cut garlic, then grease the dish with butter.

Heat the oil and half the remaining butter in a frying pan. Spread in the shallots and stir over a low heat for 5 minutes until softened. Add a little more butter, spread in the mushrooms or slivers of artichoke heart, season, and sauté for 2 to 3 minutes.

Heat the stock and wine in a small saucepan until almost simmering.

Pat the potatoes dry with a clean dish towel or paper towel. Spread a layer of potatoes in the prepared dish, half overlapping them. Season lightly. Spread a layer of shallot and mushroom or artichoke mixture. Season with a little pepper. Moisten with a little stock mixture.

Repeat until you have used all the potatoes, making sure you end with a layer of potatoes. Pour over the rest of the stock mixture. Scatter over the rest of the butter.

Bake in the oven for about 45 minutes, then turn up the heat to 400°F. Take the gratin out of the oven and scatter the blue cheese over the top. Continue baking for another 10 to 15 minutes, until the surface of the gratin is golden and the potatoes are tender – test them with a metal skewer. If the potatoes aren't quite ready, reduce the heat to its first setting and bake for another 5 to 10 minutes.

Serve hot from the dish after leaving to cool for a few minutes.

PETIT GRATIN MINUTE

FAST POTATO GRATIN

For a quick potato *gratin*, wash and scrub even-sized small but not tiny new potatoes. Cook them in lightly salted boiling water until just done. Drain and leave until cool enough to handle. Heat the broiler until very hot. Peel the potatoes if you like (I tend not to, but this is frowned on by my compatriots . . .) and cut them into slices. Butter a suitable gratin dish. Arrange the potatoes in the dish, in overlapping rows. Season generously. Scatter with grated cheese and dot with butter – the cheese is not absolutely compulsory but the butter is. Broil for 5 to 8 minutes until golden. Reduce the heat a little after 3 minutes and turn the dish around to ensure that the gratin colors evenly.

Serves 4

12-14 oz small new potatoes, well scrubbed
2-3 tbsp soft butter
⅓ cup freshly grated Gruyère or strong flavored Cheddar
sea salt and freshly ground black pepper

LEGUMES SECS, PATES ET RIZ

BEANS, LEGUMES AND PASTA

HARICOTS A LA BRETONNE

BEAN STEW WITH VEGETABLES

Serves 4 to 5 as a main
course, 6 to 8 as a side dish

1 lb haricot beans or red
kidney beans
1 bouquet garni
1 Spanish onion stuck with
3 or 4 cloves
1 small head of celery,
trimmed, washed and
chopped
3 thick slices of rindless
smoky bacon, cut into small
pieces
1 tbsp groundnut or
sunflower oil
3 tbsp butter
1 shallot, finely chopped
several leaves of lettuce,
tightly rolled and snipped
½ cup dry white wine or
apple cider
1½ tbsp finely snipped
parsley
sea salt and freshly ground
black pepper

This surprisingly fresh-tasting stew is best prepared with young haricot beans that haven't been drying on a shelf for months on end.

★ Rinse the haricot beans. Put them in a large saucepan or cooking pot, cover with plenty of cold water. Bring to the boil and simmer for 10 minutes over a moderate heat. Drain, rinse, and return to the rinsed out pan. Cover with plenty of fresh water, season lightly, and add the bouquet garni and onion stuck with a few cloves. Bring to a simmer and cook for 40 minutes, or until just tender – the timing will depend on the age of the haricot beans. After about 30 minutes, throw in the celery.

Drain well and discard the onion, cloves, and bouquet garni. Reserve the haricot beans and celery.

Meanwhile, put the chopped bacon in a large sauté or frying pan. Cover with a little boiling water and blanch for 2 minutes. Drain well and spread on a double layer of paper towels.

Heat the oil and half the butter in the pan. Spread in the shallot and lettuce and stir for 2 to 3 minutes over a low heat.

Now add the haricot beans and celery. Add the wine or cider, half the remaining butter and heat through gently, stirring from time to time.

Add to a heated serving dish. Swirl the rest of the butter in the pan and melt over moderate heat. Scatter in the bacon, stir for 2 minutes. Distribute over the dish and sprinkle with the parsley. Serve immediately.

PATES A L'ALSACIENNE

BUTTERED PASTA WITH HERBS AND CARAWAY SEEDS

Introduced into France by Catherine of Medici, pasta – *pâtes* or *nouilles* – never quite became the staple food they were in the gourmand queen's native country. Pasta made with egg yolk and generously anointed with butter is a traditional accompaniment in Alsace. In the recipe below I add a little caraway; toasted breadcrumbs (2-3 tbsp) and a sprinkling of white wine is another popular option *à l'alsacienne*.

★   In a large pan or cooking pot, bring plenty of water to the boil. Season with a teaspoon of salt and sprinkle in the oil.

Add the pasta to the boiling water and cook at a rolling boil until *al dente*. Drain well.

Swirl half the butter in the pot, add the pasta, caraway seeds. and fresh herbs. Add the rest of the butter and stir well. Serve immediately in the pot or in a heated serving dish, with a bowl of freshly grated cheese.

Serves 4

12 oz dried wide flat egg pasta such as pappardelle
1 tsp sunflower oil
3 tbsp butter
1 tsp caraway seeds
2 tbsp finely snipped mixed parsley and chives
sea salt and freshly ground black pepper
small bowl of grated Gruyère or other mature cheese, to serve

FLAGEOLETS MINUTE

A QUICK HARICOT BEAN SIDE DISH

Serves 4

*1 tbsp olive or groundnut oil
a large can of flageolets or
other haricot beans, drained
white parts of 2 large
scallions
4 tbsp dry white wine
1 tbsp diced chilled butter, or
a little more, if preferred
1 tbsp finely snipped chives
or parsley
sea salt and freshly ground
black pepper*

The Moine family's traditional accompaniment to *gigot d'agneau*. Delicious pale green *flageolets* are now relatively easy to find outside France, I am happy to say, in supermarkets and good specialist shops. Canned beans are a great stand-by – even for a (fairly) conscientious French cook. The same easy approach works well with white haricot beans, black eyed beans (add a little garlic) and kidney beans. Rinse if recommended on the can and always drain well.

★ Heat the oil in a sauté pan. Scatter the scallions in the pan and soften for 2 minutes over a low heat.

Now add the drained flageolet beans and pour in the wine. Heat through over a low heat.

Once the beans are hot, stir in the diced butter and the fresh herbs. Adjust the seasoning and serve as soon as possible.

RIZ GRATINE AUX ECHALOTES

RICE COOKED WITH SHALLOTS

Serves 4

a few drops of lemon juice
about 8 oz long-grain white rice
2 shallots, finely chopped
1 large young clove garlic
1½ tbsp extra virgin olive oil
1½ tbsp finely chopped parsley
2 oz grated Gruyère cheese
2 tbsp butter
sea salt and freshly ground black pepper

This is a typical French way of preparing rice – without fuss but with a tasty finishing touch.

★　In a large saucepan bring to the boil at least 1 quart lightly salted water. Add the lemon juice. Throw in the rice and boil uncovered for about 15 minutes or a little longer, until done to your liking.

Meanwhile, heat the oil in a small frying pan, add a tablespoon of butter. Melt, then add the shallots and garlic, and sauté over low heat for 3 to 5 minutes until softened, stirring frequently. Reserve.

Drain the rice and quickly refresh under cold water, drain again. Use at once or set aside until about 20 minutes before you are ready to eat.

Heat the oven to 350°F. Using half the remaining butter, grease a gratin dish. Put the rice in the dish, season, and stir in the shallots, garlic, and parsley.

Sprinkle over the grated cheese, dot with the rest of the butter and bake in the oven for 10 to 15 minutes until golden and piping hot. Serve as soon as possible.

LENTILLES EN COCOTTE

LENTIL CASSEROLE WITH ONION AND TOMATOES

Serves 4

*12 oz small dark lentils,
rinsed and drained
1½ tbsp olive oil
1 large sweet white onion,
finely chopped
1 clove garlic, crushed
about 2 cups chicken or
vegetable stock
1 bouquet garni
a small can of tomatoes, well
drained and chopped
1 tsp dried ground thyme
½ tsp each dried rubbed sage
and marjoram
3 thick slices of rindless
smoky bacon, cut into small
pieces, blanched and drained
(see page 52, Bean Stew)
1 tbsp finely snipped parsley
sea salt and freshly ground
black pepper*

Lentils have always been a popular legume in France. I am always amazed to see how quickly they can turn from an elegant concoction into a stodgy mush. The secret is twofold: choose good quality small dark lentils (Le Puy is probably the best provenance) and err on the side of undercooking. Lentils taste best still a little firm.

With or without bacon, *Lentilles en cocotte* make a good accompaniment to meaty spicy sausages and, yes, roast chicken.

★ In a sauté pan heat half of the oil until hot. Add the onion and sauté for 2 to 3 minutes over low heat, stirring occasionally. Stir the garlic and lentils into the softened onion. Cover with the stock (and top off with water if necessary): you should have about 1 inch of liquid above the lentils.

Season, add the bouquet garni, tomatoes, and dried herbs. Bring to a simmer. Reduce the heat a little, half cover, and simmer over a low heat for 25 to 35 minutes, until the lentils are just tender but not at all soft. Stir from time to time – add a tablespoon or two of water or stock if the lentil mixture looks dry.

When the lentils are cooked, heat the rest of the oil in a small frying pan. Sauté the blanched bacon for 2 minutes until crisp. Reserve.

Drain the lentils and discard the bouquet garni. Put into a heated serving dish. Adjust the seasoning. Scatter over the sautéed bacon and the parsley. Serve hot.

LIST OF RECIPES